JOANNE OPPENHEIM

●

RON BRODA

HAVE YOU
SEEN
BUGS?

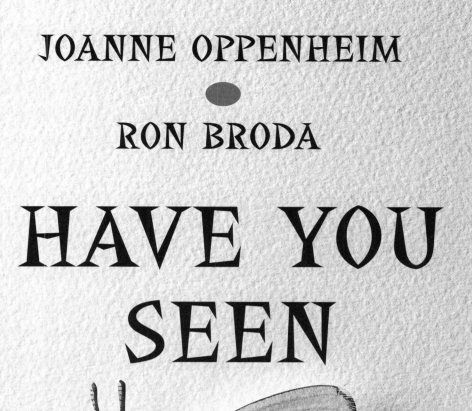

BUGS?

North Winds Press
A Division of Scholastic Canada Ltd.

To Toni.
— J.O.

To my own little bugs,
Taylor and Eden Broda.
— R.B.

The illustrator would like to thank Joanne Webb
for her help with page 30 — what a great idea! Thanks also to William Kuryluk
fo a wonderful job on the photography.

The illustrations for this book were made with paper sculpture and watercolour.
Each layer of paper was cut, formed and painted before being glued into place.
The finished sculptures were then carefully lit and photographed to create
the final image.

Photography by William Kuryluk.

Canadian Cataloguing in Publication Data
Oppenheim, Joanne
Have you seen bugs?

ISBN 0-590-24322-5

1. Insects - Juvenile literature. I. Broda, Ron.
II. Title.
QL467.2.O66 1996   J595.7   C95-932994-3

7 6 5 4 3 2 1   Printed in Canada   6 7 8 9 / 9

Have you seen bugs?

Itty-bitty bugs
small as specks of sand,

wide-winged bugs
bigger than your hand.

2

Bugs with stripes
or speckles
or spots,
shiny like metal
or covered with dots.

Iridescent bugs
that shimmer in the light,

winking, blinking bugs
that twinkle in the night.

Dark as bark
green as grass
see-through bugs
with wings like glass.

Shaped like thorns
or sticks
or leaves,

burrowed in bubbles
or clinging to trees.

Hide-and-seek bugs —
can you see these?

6

Watch out! for these show-off bugs
with colours bold and bright.
Flashy, sassy, daring bugs
such easy bugs to sight!

Like warning signs,
bold markings say:
I'm poison! I smell!
I stink! Stay away!

Have you seen bugs
and how they move?

Long-legged bugs
jumping with a bound,
short-legged bugs
running on the ground.

Some are fast:
they dart and leap;
some are slow:
they crawl and creep.

Bugs that flutter
    and scurry
        and dive,
bugs that buzz around a hive.

Walking on the ceiling,
crawling up a wall —
some bugs hardly move at all!

What about water bugs?
Walking-on-the-water bugs
swimming-under-water bugs
skimming-over-water bugs.

Oaring, soaring,
    whirling, twirling,
        striding, gliding.
Have you seen these?

Have you heard bugs?

Bugs have no voices
but still they can sing,
rubbing their legs,
whirring their wings.

16

Busy crickets in thickets
wait for night to fall,
then they rub their legs together
and chirp their mating call.

A bug has no ears
on its little bug head,
but some bugs hear
through their legs instead!
While others use antennae

to taste and hear and smell,
and tiny hairs that touch and tell
and help them find their mates as well.
Some bugs even use their feet
to take a taste before they eat!

Have you seen bugs
and how they eat?

Beetles have mouths —
they can bite and chew and snip,
while others like the butterfly
have mouths with straws that sip.

20

Most bugs dine on plants,
some bugs dine on meat,
others take a nip of blood
or sip on nectar sweet.

Have you seen baby bugs?

Inside a hive,
nesting in hair,

bugs hatch from eggs
everywhere.

Underwater, underground,
in so many places
bug eggs are found.

In the bark of trees
or wrapped up in leaves,
baby bugs hatch
from all of these!

Baby bugs are small,
but just for a bit.
Little bugs keep growing
till their skins don't fit.

24

But some bugs form a chrysalis
or spin a fine cocoon,
where abracadabra! they grow wide wings
in a magical changing room.

25

Have you seen working bugs?
From flower to flower,
bugs work as they go,

carrying pollen
that makes gardens grow.
If it weren't for bugs,
orchards would be bare!
You couldn't have an apple,
    an orange or a pear.
There wouldn't be corn
    or pumpkins or wheat;
without bugs we'd have little to eat.

26

Burrowing, weaving
or building a nest,
gathering, guarding,
seldom at rest,

working by day,
working by night,
spinning wondrous webs
or taking off in flight.

Sleek as a needle,
furry as a bear,
so many kinds of bugs
living everywhere!

An army of ants
a flurry of fleas
a band of moths
a swarm of bees
billions of bugs . . .

Have you seen these?

ABOUT BUGS

Some bugs are insects,
others are not.
Compare their bodies
to find what you've got:
    An insect has three parts —
        a head at one end
        an abdomen in the rear
        a thorax in the middle
        where wings and legs appear.
    An insect has six legs,
no fewer and no more;
some have two wings
but many have four.
Some primitive insects have no wings at all,
like lice or fleas — they hop or crawl.

The bugs in this book are all arthropods. They include insects (class Insecta), spiders (class Arachnida) and millipedes (class Diplopoda).

Can you see these bugs?

The bugs in the text areas are listed from top to bottom; the ones in the pictures are listed from left to right.

Page 1 Colorado potato beetle, searcher, yellow woolly bear, white-marked tussock moth, red ant worker, fall cankerworm, anise swallowtail, short-stalked damselfly, rough fungus beetle, oblong-winged katydid, aphid, golden garden spider

Pages 2-3 Text area: Costa Rican beetle, cotton-wood borer; Picture: stag beetle, ladybug, polyphemus moth, ten-lined June beetle

Pages 4-5 Text area: lichen moth, *Brochymena*; Picture: musk beetle, fire bug, apple-sucker, ant lion fly, green lacewing, firefly, green stink bug, darkling beetle

Pages 6-7 Text area: acraea moth, big poplar sphinx; Picture: titan stick insect, California canker-worm moth, treehopper, spittlebug, locust treehopper, eastern tiger swallowtail, northern walking stick, true katydid, leaf insect, Nebraska conehead

Pages 8-9 zebra longwing, blister beetle

Pages 10-11 Text area: tropical lubber grasshopper, weevil; Picture: tropical millipede, ear-wig, praying mantis, question mark, silverfish

Pages 12-13 green darner, red skimmer, black horsefly

Pages 14-15 European water spider, backswimmer, water strider, house mosquito larvae and pupae, small whirligig beetle, western mountain gomphid dragonfly, water stick insect, golden mayfly

Pages 16-17 Text area: periodical cicada, click beetle; Picture: Mormon cricket

Pages 18-19 male African moon moth

Pages 20-21 Text area: *Nessaea aglaura;* Picture: nine-spotted ladybug beetle, summer mosquito

Pages 22-23 field cricket and eggs, golden garden spider and egg sac, tomato hornworm moth with braconid wasp cocoons on its back, lacewing eggs, may beetle larva, harlequin cabbage bug and eggs, lady beetle eggs, honey bee eggs, larvae, drones, workers, queen

Pages 24-25 monarch butterfly — caterpillar, chrysalis, adult

Pages 26-27 Text area: shamrock spider, bark beetle tunnels; Picture: crater-nest ant, honey bee

Pages 28-29 Text area: privet hawkmoth caterpillar, golden northern bumblebee; Picture: garden spider

Page 30 All the bugs on this page can be found elsewhere in the book — except for one mystery bug invented by the illustrator. Can you spot the fake?